Hindu
holy days

Offerings at a temple.

Lisa Magloff

Glossary

AARTI A type of prayer in which light, in the form of burning candles, incense and other items are offered as a thanks and worship to God. In temples, aarti is usually performed three times each day.

DURGA A form of the goddess Parvati, who is the wife of Lord Shiva. She protects people from evil and misery by destroying evil forces such as selfishness, jealousy, prejudice, hatred and anger. Durga is also thought of as mother nature.

GANESHA The elephant-headed son of the god Shiva and the goddess Parvati, and the god of wisdom. He is also called 'the remover of obstacles' and so he is worshipped before starting any new venture.

GODS AND GODDESSES Hindus believe in one God, but they believe that God has many different forms, or parts, called gods and goddesses and that worshipping any god or goddess is the same as worshipping God.

HOLY SCRIPTURE Books of religious teachings and stories. There are many different Hindu scriptures. The two main groups are shruti, believed to have come directly from God, and smitri, which were composed long ago by scholars and poets.

HYMN A religious song or a song with a religious meaning.

KALI Another form or part of the goddess Lakshmi. But Kali is the part of Lakshmi that destroys evil and demons. Kali also stands for the fear that must be overcome before we can become closer to God.

KRISHNA A form of the god Vishnu. Krishna stands for joy, freedom and love. He is often shown as a mischievous child and many stories in the Hindu scriptures are told of his childhood. In his adult life, Krishna was the wise hero of the ancient epic, the Mahabharata, and he laid down the basic ideas of practical Hinduism. Krishna is also believed to have spoken the Bhagavad Gita, the most famous scripture of the Hindus.

LAKSHMI The wife of Lord Vishnu and the goddess of wealth, prosperity, beauty and good luck.

LORD Another name for God.

OFFERING A gift left for a god or goddess. Almost anything can be an offering, such as food, prayers or song. Hindus believe that the gods bless the offerings and the giver.

RAMA AND SITA The story of Rama and Sita is told in Hindu holy scripture. Rama was a part of the god Vishnu and the prince of the kingdom of Ayodhya, and Sita was his wife. The scripture, the Ramayana, tells the story of their adventures. The stories of Rama and Sita teach the proper way for kings to behave to their subjects, and how husbands and wives should treat each other, and how to be faithful to our family and those we love. The stories emphasise that proper behaviour by everyone in society will lead to peace and harmony for all.

RANGOLI A design made from coloured sand or grains of rice. The designs are made in doorways and other places as a way to celebrate festivals. They are usually brushed away as part of the celebration.

SHRINE The shrine can be thought of as the home of the god or goddess. Prayers are said and offerings are left in front of the shrine. Temples usually have many shrines, and most Hindu homes will have a shrine for daily worship. Inside the shrine are statues or paintings of a god or goddess.

Contents

As you go through the book, look for words in **BOLD CAPITALS**. These words are defined in the glossary.

 Understanding others

Remember that other people's beliefs are important to them. You must always be considerate and understanding when studying about faith.

Worshippers celebrate a holy day with music and prayer.

What is a holy day?

As in other faiths, Hindu holidays celebrate important events in the year.

People of all faiths worship throughout the whole year. But in all faiths, some days are special. These special days, or holy days, may remember an important event in the history of the faith, or they may remember events or stories described in **HOLY SCRIPTURE** (writings).

These holy days are different from a day of rest and worship that many religions have each week. Many holy days involve public celebrations, special meals, festivals and even processions. In general, we call these special days holy days and it is from this that we get the word 'holiday'.

In the Hindu faith there is no weekly day of rest. Many Hindus pray at home every day, and go to the temple whenever they want to.

There are, however, hundreds of holy days in the Hindu faith. Not everyone celebrates each one. Instead, people celebrate the holy days that mean the most to them. Some, like Diwali, are celebrated by Hindus all over the world, while others are celebrated only by a few people.

Some of the Hindu holidays remember important events in the lives of the **GODS AND GODDESSES**. Others celebrate the harvest, the start of the planting season, or another yearly event.

As you look at the main holy days of the Hindu faith in this book, notice how there are many different ways to mark out or celebrate each day.

◀ Many celebrations involve eating special foods.

▲ Worship in a temple or at a SHRINE is an important part of holy day celebrations.

▲ Many Hindu holy day celebrations include leaving OFFERINGS for the gods and goddesses.

The Hindu holy day calendar

Here are the parts of the year when Hindu holidays occur. The actual date varies from one year to another.

Today, many people in the world use a calendar which divides the year into 12 months and begins on January 1. In this calendar, the Sun is used as a guide and one year is about the time it takes the Earth to move around the Sun.

But not all calendars look like this. Some calendars, for example, use the way the Moon moves across the sky as a guide. There are many different Hindu calendars, but most of them are organised like this. Because there are different Hindu calendars, some holidays may be celebrated on different days in different places.

Months of the Indian Calendar		
1	**Chaitra**	Mar 20/21* to April 20
2	**Vaisakha**	April 21 to May 21
3	**Jyaistha**	May 22 to June 21
4	**Asadha**	June 22 to July 22
5	**Shravana**	July 23 to Aug 22
6	**Bhadra**	Aug 23 to Sept 22
7	**Asvina**	Sept 23 to Oct 22
8	**Kartika**	Oct 23 to Nov 21
9	**Agrahayana**	Nov 22 to Dec 21
10	**Pausa**	Dec 22 to Jan 20
11	**Magha**	Jan 21 to Feb 19
12	**Phalguna**	Feb 20 to Mar 19/20

▲ This calendar is the main Hindu calendar. It is the one used by the government of India. It is based on both lunar and solar years. (*In leap years Chaitra starts on March 21.*)

◀ A Hindu girl celebrates.

▶ In this chart, you can see how the Hindu holy days are spread around the year, and how the days move around a little from year to year.

HINDU HOLY DAYS

	2007	2008	2009	2010	2011
Holi	Mar 4	Mar 22	Mar 11	Mar 1	Mar 20
Ganesh Chaturthi	Sept 15	Sept 3	Aug 23	Sept 11	Sept 1
Dusshera	Oct 21	Oct 9	Sept 28	Oct 17	Oct 6
Maghi	Oct 12	Sept 30	Sept 19	Oct 8	Sept 28
Diwali	Nov 9	Oct 28	Oct 17	Nov 5	Oct 26
Makar Sankrati	Jan 14	Jan 14	Jan 14	Jan 14	Jan 14
Janmashtami	Sept 4	Aug 24	Aug 14	Sept 2	Aug 22

A New Year holiday

The holiday of Holi is celebrated during the month of Phalguna (February to March).

The spring festival of Holi welcomes in the New Year. It is a time to celebrate the new life of spring.

Holi is also a time to worship the **LORD** Vishnu. Hindu holy scripture tells about how a boy named Prahlada was saved from an evil demon named Holika because he worshipped Vishnu. This story is told on Holi as a reminder of how Vishnu protects people from evil.

The story of Holika and Prahlada

Once there was a cruel and wicked king, who thought that he was so important, that all his people should worship him, just as if he were a god. The king had a son called Prahlada. Prahlada knew that his own father was not a god and that it was wrong to worship him, so Prahlada worshipped Lord Vishnu instead.

One day the king asked Prahlada, "Who is the greatest, God or I?"

Prahlada answered, "God is greater, you are only a king." The king was furious when he heard this answer and he had Prahlada thrown into a pit full of hissing snakes. But Lord Vishnu protected Prahlada and he came out of the snake-pit without a bite.

Then the king grew even more furious and ordered his son to be trampled on by a herd of elephants. But again Lord Vishnu protected Prahlada and he was unharmed.

Finally, the king asked his sister, Holika, to kill Prahlada. Holika had been given a magic power by the gods so that she could never be burnt by fire, so she grabbed Prahlada and held him in the middle of a huge bonfire.

But when the gods saw that Holika was using her power to do something evil, they took the power away. Lord Vishnu protected Prahlada from the fire, while Holika burnt up. So Prahlada, who put his faith in Vishnu, was saved.

During Holi, Hindus tell this story to help them remember that good is always more powerful than evil and that people who believe in God will always be safe.

Celebrating Krishna

Holi also celebrates the god Lord **KRISHNA**. One very popular Holi custom comes from Lord Krishna's life. According to tradition, when Lord Krishna was a young man he fell in love with a milkmaid named Radha.

One day, Lord Krishna told his mother that he was worried because Radha was very fair and he was very dark. Krishna's mother told him to throw coloured water onto Radha's face and she would look darker. Krishna did this, but Radha did not like it, so she threw coloured water all over Krishna.

Holi celebrations

The festival of Holi lasts for two days, and most of the celebrations take place outside.

◄ In many places, huge bonfires are lit to celebrate the festival of Holi. The bonfires are a reminder of how the evil Holika tried to burn Prahlada in a fire.

◀ These people are preparing offerings of grains and coconut to be burned in the bonfire.

On the first night, huge bonfires are lit. This is a reminder of the story of Prahlada and Holika. It is also a reminder of the coming of spring.

Food, such as grains and coconut, are roasted on the bonfire as offerings to Lord Vishnu. Hindus believe that burning the grains and coconut stand for the casting away of sins.

The most popular way to celebrate Holi is by throwing coloured water onto other people. This remembers the story of Krishna and Radha. Everyone participates in throwing coloured water. Many people dress in white, so the colours show up better, and everyone is prepared to get covered in coloured water, dye and powders.

Holi is a time for fun and enjoyment in public. In India, there may be music and dancing in the streets and large festivals and fêtes. In the UK, the celebrations may be smaller and may be held in a temple or community centre, but they are just as much fun.

◀ The coconuts will be burned as a symbol of casting off sins.

Ganesh Chaturthi

This holiday takes place on the fourth day of Bhadra (August to September) and celebrates the birthday of the god Ganesha.

GANESHA is one of the most popular Hindu gods. He is the son of the god Shiva and the goddess Parvati.

Ganesha is the god of wisdom and he also protects people by removing obstacles and difficulties and by bringing good luck. The holiday of Ganesh Chaturthi celebrates Ganesha's birthday. Because Ganesha is so popular, his birthday is celebrated by a very large number of Hindus all over the world.

The story of Ganesha's birth

One day while the goddess Parvati was bathing, she created a boy out of mud and gave him the job of guarding the entrance to her bathroom.

When Parvati's husband, Shiva, came home, he was surprised to find a strange boy keeping him out. When the boy refused to let him enter the bathroom, Shiva grew very angry and cut off the boy's head. As soon as Parvati saw this she became very upset. In order to calm Parvati, Shiva sent his guards to fetch the head of any sleeping human or animal that was facing north. The guards returned with an elephant's head.

Shiva brought Ganesha back to life and attached the elephant's head to his body. Then Shiva told Ganesha that for all time, people would pray to him before starting anything new.

During the holiday, children are told the story of how Ganesha was born, and how he came to have an elephant's head.

Ganesh Chaturthi and the Moon

One tradition on Ganesh Chaturthi is that it is bad luck to look at the Moon. This story tells why.

Ganesha is very fond of a sweet called a ladoo. On his birthday, Ganesha likes to go around from house to house accepting the offerings of ladoos that people leave for him. As he goes around, Ganesha rides on a mouse.

One year after he had eaten a lot of ladoos, the mouse saw a snake and stumbled and Ganesha fell down.

Ganesha fell so hard that his stomach burst and all the ladoos came tumbling out. But Ganesha stuffed them back into his stomach, caught hold of the snake and tied it around his belly like a belt.

Seeing all this, the Moon in the sky began to laugh. This annoyed Ganesha terribly and so he pulled out one of his tusks and hurled it against the Moon, and said that no one should look at the Moon on Ganesh Chaturthi day. If anyone does, he will surely earn bad luck.

◀ Ganesha with a bowl of ladoo sweets. These are said to be Ganesha's favourite food. They are made from sweetened milk curds.

Celebrating Ganesh Chaturthi

There are many different ways to celebrate this holiday, but they all include offering prayers, **HYMNS** and special foods to Ganesha. Because Hindu tradition says that Ganesha is very fond of sweets, his birthday celebrations also include giving gifts of specially-made sweets.

The holiday usually lasts for several days. Before it begins, families and temples make or buy very large statues of Ganesha made out of clay or papier mâché. These statues are painted and decorated with flowers, clothing and lights. Hindus believe that, during the holiday, Ganesha comes down and lives in the statues so that he can celebrate his birthday with everyone.

▼ Ganesha statues made out of clay.

▲ Traditional music is an important part of many holiday celebrations.

▲ A statue of Ganesha is dressed and decorated in preparation for a procession to celebrate Ganesh Chaturthi.

Throughout the holiday, people offer prayers, hymns, music and food to the statues of Ganesha. In this way, everybody has a chance to celebrate with Ganesha.

In the UK, temples may also organise festivals or fêtes. These can include prayers, singing, dancing, talks about the Hindu religion, games, meals and even artistic and fancy dress competitions.

At the end of the holiday, the statues may be paraded through the streets as part of a big procession. They are then immersed in a river or the ocean. When the clay or papier mâché statues are placed in the water at the end of the holiday, the statues break apart and Ganesha returns to his home with the gods and goddesses.

Durga Puja and Dusshera

This nine day holiday celebrates the goddess Durga. It ends with a holiday remembering how the god Rama killed an evil king.

The holiday of Durga Puja, Dusshera, or Navaratri, lasts for nine days and takes place in the month of Asvina (September/October). During this holiday, Hindus worship the goddess **DURGA**, who protects people from evil by destroying evil forces such as anger and hatred.

Because Durga is worshipped as the part of God that protects life, she is sometimes called the Mother Goddess, or Divine Mother. Other goddesses, such as **LAKSHMI** and Saraswati, are also worshipped during Durga Puja.

The story of Durga

Long ago, there was a powerful demon king named Mahisha. Mahisha prayed to Brahma to become immortal. Brahma told Mahisha that he could not grant immortality. But Brahma blessed Mahisha so that he could only be killed by a woman.

Mahisha then drove away the gods from heaven and took over the throne of their king, Indra. Finally, the gods joined forces to create the goddess Durga.

After a battle lasting for nine days and nights, Durga killed Mahisha and brought peace back to Earth.

Every year, Durga comes to Earth for ten days. During this time, Hindus celebrate the victory of Durga over Mahisha.

Durga Puja traditions

There are many different traditions for celebrating and worshipping during Durga Puja, but all of them include worshipping Durga.

One of the most popular is to make a special shrine, called a golu, at home.

◀▲ The goddess Durga is usually shown with eight arms and seated on a tiger.

The shrine usually has seven or nine steps, and on each step are statues of gods and goddesses. Families worship in front of the golu each day during the holiday.

Many families also celebrate by sharing festive meals with family and friends. There may also be community concerts, dances and fêtes.

Another tradition during Durga Puja is to make huge statues of Durga out of papier mâché and then carry them through the streets in a procession, accompanied by music and hymns.

Some Hindus may also plant nine different kinds of food seeds, such as rice, barley or vegetables, in small containers on the first day of Durga Puja. The plants are watered each day and by the ninth day they have sprouted. The sprouts are then placed on the golu as an offering to Durga.

The holiday may also be spent in fasting and in prayer. People ask Durga to protect their health and their family.

For many people, Durga Puja is also seen as a time of good luck and a good time to begin new things.

Dusshera

Durga Puja lasts for nine days. On the tenth day is a holiday called Dusshera, or Dassera.

According to Hindu tradition, the holiday of Dusshera was started by Lord Rama. The story of Lord Rama is told in the Hindu holy scripture called the Ramayana.

Celebrating Dusshera

Just like Durga Puja, there are many different ways to celebrate Dusshera. One way is by telling the story of **RAMA AND SITA**. In temples there may be talks or lectures about the meaning of the story.

Rama was a great warrior king who was heir to the kingdom of Ayodhya. But Rama's stepmother did not want him on the throne and she convinced Rama's father, the king, to exile Rama to the forest, along with his wife Sita and his younger brother Lakshman.

While in the forest, Sita was carried off by Ravana, the demon king of Lanka. Rama decided to rescue Sita. Before fighting Ravana, Rama spent nine days praying to Durga. On the tenth day, he defeated Ravana and rescued Sita. The holiday of Dusshera celebrates this event.

Hindu tradition says that any new venture started on Dusshera will be successful. So, many people choose to open new businesses or start projects at this time.

In some families, things that are important for work and school, such as tools, writing instruments, machines, household articles and children's school books are placed in front of a statue of Durga, so the goddess can bless them.

Many families also share festive meals with friends and relatives, while communities around the world organise dances and fêtes. These might take place in Hindu temples or community centres. There may also be fireworks or bonfires, where papier mâché statues of Ravana are burnt.

▲ The story of Lord Rama and his wife Sita is told on Dusshera.

▶ Burning papier mâché statues of the evil demon Ravana is a popular way to celebrate Dusshera. However people celebrate, Dusshera is always a happy and joyous time.

Krishna's birthday

The holiday of Krishna Janmashtami, or Sri Krishna Jayanti, celebrates the birth of Krishna. It usually occurs in August or September.

▼ Acting out the story of Lord Krishna.

Lord Krishna is one of the most popular Hindu gods, and so his birthday is an important holiday for the many Hindus who worship him.

Janmashtami (also known as Sri Krishna Jayanti) is celebrated over two days. On the first day, many people fast until midnight. They may spend the day in prayer and go to the temple to look at statues of Lord Krishna and leave offerings. In homes, people often place a small statue of baby Krishna in a cradle.

At midnight there are prayers and an **AARTI** ceremony, followed by a special feast. Lord Krishna was a cow herd when he was a boy, and loved to eat milk and butter, so many foods made from milk and curds are served at the feast.

The second day

In ancient times, Indian farmers used to hang pots of food from the roof in order to prevent animals from eating them. One story told about Lord Krishna is that every day after the men and women left for their farms, the naughty and adventurous Krishna and his friends would build a human pyramid and steal milk and butter from the hanging pots.

So, on the second day of Janmashtami, some Hindus remember this story with a contest called dahi-handi. A large earthenware pot is filled with milk, curds, butter, honey and fruits and is hung from the ceiling. Children and adults compete to claim the prize by building a human pyramid.

Other celebrations

On Janmashtami there are also large fêtes and festivals. Decorations showing Krishna's birth are displayed and plays about Lord Krishna's birth and boyhood are put on.

▲▼ Decorated statues of Lord Krishna.

Diwali

This holiday is celebrated by Hindus all over the world.

Diwali is on the New Moon in the month of Kartika (October to November), but celebrations usually begin a few days before the New Moon and last for several days. During Diwali, Hindus celebrate two different things: the goddess Lakshmi, and the idea that good will always defeat evil.

Diwali is a time for Hindus to welcome the goddess Lakshmi into their homes. Lakshmi is the goddess of wealth, and Hindus hope that a visit from her means they will have good fortune for the rest of the year.

Diwali is also a time to celebrate the idea that good always defeats evil. So, on Diwali, Hindus remember stories from Hindu holy scripture about how good will always defeat evil.

Story of Diwali

During Diwali, many stories are told about the gods and goddesses defeating evil demons. The most popular is the story of how Rama and Sita returned to Ayodhya after being exiled to a forest for 14 years and defeating the demon Ravana.

Happy Diwali

Diwali is derived from the Sanskrit word, Deepawali, "Deep" meaning light and "avali" meaning a row. As India is such a diverse country, this most celebrated Indian festival symbolises unity, prosperity and happiness

▼ The goddess Lakshmi is worshipped on Diwali.

After defeating Ravana, Rama, Sita and Lakshman returned to Ayodhya. It was a dark moonless night and they couldn't see where they were going. The people put little lamps outside their houses so that the new king and queen could find their way, and to welcome Rama, Sita and Lakshman home.

Overjoyed at Queen Sita's rescue and the safe return of King Rama, the people danced and celebrated and lit fireworks to show how happy they were.

Each year during Diwali, Hindus celebrate the return to Ayodhya with festivals and fireworks. The word Diwali is a short version of the word Deepavali, which means 'rows of lights' and Diwali is often called 'The festival of lights'.

▼▶ Fireworks and a firecracker for Diwali.

▼ Traditional clay lamps are lit as a reminder of Rama and Sita's return to Ayodhya.

Weblink: www.CurriculumVisions.com

Other Diwali stories

Many other stories about the gods and goddesses are told on Diwali. Most of these stories tell how different gods and goddesses defeated evil. One popular story tells of how Lord Krishna defeated the demon Narakasura.

The meaning of the stories

All of the stories show people that good (Rama, Krishna and **KALI**) will always be able to defeat evil (Ravana, Narakasura and Raktabija).

So, Diwali celebrates not only the happy ending of the stories, but also the idea that good can overcome evil.

How Lord Krishna defeated Narakasura

The demon Narakasura was a powerful and evil king. Narakasura even believed that he was as powerful as the gods and could do what he liked. He kidnapped 16,000 daughters of the gods, and stole the earrings of Aditi, mother of the gods.

The gods asked the god Krishna for help. Krishna and Narakasura fought a great battle, which ended when Krishna killed the demon, freed the girls and recovered the earrings.

After his victory Krishna returned very early in the morning and was bathed and massaged with scented oils. Taking an early morning bath with oil is still a Diwali tradition.

▶ Krishna.

How Kali killed Raktabija

Raktabija was an evil demon. The gods tried to kill him, but every time a drop of his blood fell to the ground, it turned into another Raktabija. Soon there were millions of demon Raktabijas.

The gods turned to Shiva for help, but Shiva was praying and he did not hear them. So the gods turned to Shiva's wife, Parvati, for help.

Parvati agreed to help and turned herself into Kali, the goddess who destroys evil. When the gods attacked Raktabija, Kali spread her tongue over the whole battlefield, covering it completely, so none of the demon's blood could fall to the ground. No new demons could be made and the gods were finally able to destroy Raktabija.

◀ Kali.

Look forward to better things as you celebrate the auspicious occasion of Diwali.

▲ Diwali cards.

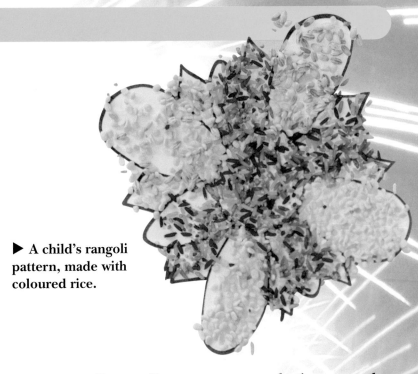

▶ A child's rangoli pattern, made with coloured rice.

Diwali celebrations

The holiday of Diwali is usually celebrated for five days.

On the first day, families clean and decorate their homes and get ready to welcome Lakshmi. People may also send out 'Happy Diwali' cards to family and friends. In some houses, RANGOLI patterns are drawn on the floors to welcome Lakshmi.

Rangoli patterns are designs made from coloured rice powder, sand or crushed chalk. They are drawn with the fingers. Some families also draw footprints leading up to their door, to show Lakshmi the way in.

▼ This peacock is a rangoli pattern made from coloured sand.

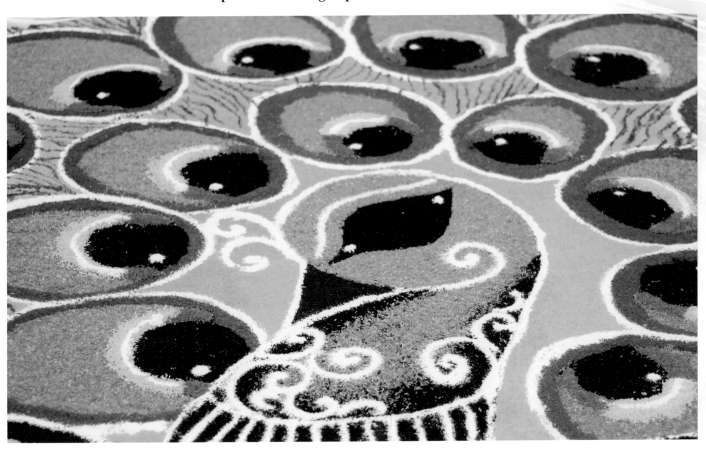

▲ Hindus attend worship services at temples during Diwali.

Each day during Diwali, families gather in the evening at home shrines to offer Lakshmi and Rama prayers, songs and offerings of sweets.

After worship, oil lamps, called diyas, are lit and placed around the house. Each night during Diwali, candles and lamps are lit in homes, temples and other buildings as a greeting to Lakshmi and Rama.

On the second day of the holiday, some people celebrate by taking a bath with scented oil in the water. This is a reminder of the bath that Krishna took after he killed the demon Narakasura.

▼ Many kinds of lanterns are lit during Diwali celebrations.

▲ Offerings of traditional sweets for Diwali.

The third day of Diwali is the main celebration. Many people go to their temple, where there are worship services for Lakshmi. All through the evening people let off firecrackers. Families and friends gather for festive meals, and people meet friends and neighbours to exchange good wishes and presents.

On the fifth day of Diwali, one tradition is for sisters to put a dot of coloured, scented paste, called a tilaka, on their brother's forehead. The sisters then pray for their brother to have a long and happy life.

▼ Floating lanterns at a Diwali celebration in Trafalgar Square, London.

Harvest festivals

January is the time for one of the largest Hindu harvest festivals.

Hindus celebrate many different harvest festivals at different times of the year. This is because Hinduism began in India and India is a large country, so the harvests come at different times of the year in different places.

One of the most popular Hindu harvest festivals begins on January 14 every year and celebrates the winter harvest.

This festival has many names, such as Makar Sankrati, Pongal or Lohri, and is celebrated in many different ways. For some people, the celebrations last for four days, while for others they only last one day. But for everyone, this is a joyous and happy time, and a time to thank God for the harvest.

Four day celebrations

In southern India, the harvest holiday is called Pongal and lasts for four days.

On the first day families offer prayers to the god Indra, who is the king of the gods and also the god of

◄▲► During Pongal, rice and milk are boiled together until they overflow the pot. This stands for the hope that the harvest will be plentiful.

clouds and rain. Houses are cleaned and decorated with designs called kolams that are made out of coloured rice flour and painted on the floor.

The word 'ponga' means 'to boil', and on each day of Pongal, rice and milk are cooked together in a new pot until the rice boils over the top of the pot.

► Fried rice balls are a popular food during the harvest festival.

The second day of Pongal is a time to worship Surya, the god of the Sun. In temples and homes, people place offerings of sugarcane and festive foods in front of statues of Surya.

The third day of Pongal is a time to celebrate cattle. Farmers give thanks for their cows by painting their horns and tying bells around their necks.

In temples and at home, people offer prayers to Ganesha and the goddess Parvati.

On the fourth day people travel to visit their families. Families have festive meals together and children are given small gifts.

▼ During Pongal, farmers in India decorate their cows as a way to give thanks for the gifts the cows bring, such as milk, cheese and yoghurt.

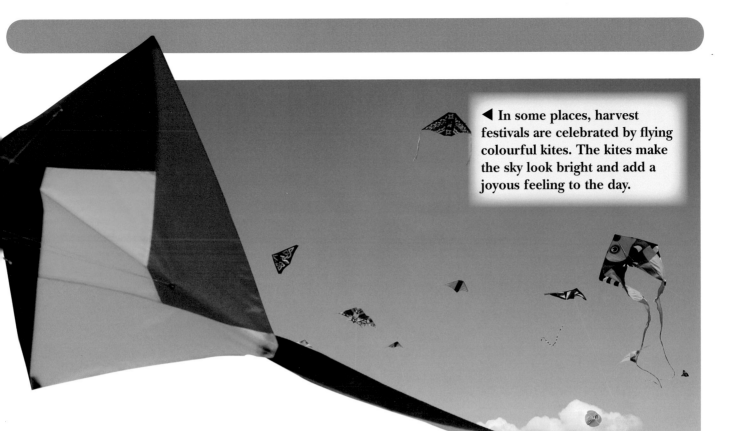

In some places, harvest festivals are celebrated by flying colourful kites. The kites make the sky look bright and add a joyous feeling to the day.

Celebrating in other ways

In Punjab, where winter is the coldest month of the year, the harvest festival is called Lohri and is celebrated with huge bonfires. Each neighbourhood builds a bonfire. Sweets, sugarcane and rice are thrown into the fire as offerings, and prayers of thanks are said. Families have festive meals and people give friends and family gifts of sweets. According to tradition, if everyone has a good time on Lohri, then the rest of the year will also be good.

In Rajasthan, Maharashtra and Gujarat the harvest holiday is called Makar Sankrati and is celebrated by giving gifts to friends and relatives. In some places, people celebrate by flying colourful kites.

In Uttar Pradesh, the holiday is called Kicheri and is celebrated with fêtes and outdoor festivals.

It is considered important to have a bath on this day, and many people go to bathe in sacred rivers.

The meaning of harvest festivals

Although the harvest holiday is celebrated in many different ways, you can see that it is always a happy time.

In the UK, celebrations may be simpler than in India and may take place at home or in a temple.

But wherever the harvest holiday is celebrated, it always includes making offerings to the gods and goddesses. This is a way to say thank you to God for the harvest. The celebrations also usually include giving gifts of food or festive meals. This is a way of sharing the blessings of God with family and friends.

Index

(Curriculum Visions)

You might also be interested in
'Hindu mandir', 'Hindu faith and practice' and 'Hindu art and writing'.

Dedicated Web Site
Much more in detail can be found at:
www.curriculumvisions.com
(Subscription required)

A CVP Book
Copyright © 2007–2011 Atlantic Europe Publishing

First reprint 2011

The right of Lisa Magloff to be identified as the author of this work has been asserted by her in accordance with the Copyright, Designs and Patents Act 1988.

Author
Lisa Magloff, MA

Religious Adviser
Radha Mohan Bhaktivedanta Manor

Senior Designer
Adele Humphries, BA

Acknowledgements
The publishers would like to thank everyone at the Bhaktivedanta Manor, Dharam Marg, Hilfield Lane, Aldenham, Herts for their help and advice.

Photographs
The Earthscape Picture Library, except: (c=centre, t=top, b=bottom, l=left, r=right) pages 12, 14 (Ganesha statues), 15, 17, 18, 23tr, 25b, 26cl, 30, 31 *ShutterStock*; pages 13, 26–27 *UK Student Life*; pages 25tl and 26bl *(Diwali sweets) DHD Multimedia Gallery*; pages 19, 20, 21t *Bhaktivedanta Manor.*

Illustrations
David Woodroffe

Designed and produced by
Atlantic Europe Publishing

Printed in China by
WKT Company Ltd

Hindu holy days
– Curriculum Visions
A CIP record for this book is available from the British Library
ISBN: 978 1 86214 502 3

This product is manufactured from sustainable managed forests. For every tree cut down at least one more is planted.